Manage Your World
on
ONE PAGE

Align and Motivate People

Stay Focused

Manage Complexity

Communicate Priorities

DR. STEPHEN G. PAYNE   ALAN S.W. DOWIE

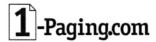 -Paging.com

AuthorHouse™
1663 Liberty Drive, Suite 200
Bloomington, IN 47403
www.authorhouse.com
Phone: 1-800-839-8640

First published by AuthorHouse 1/18/2008

ISBN: 978-1-4343-5941-4 (sc)

Printed in the United States of America
Bloomington, Indiana

This book is printed on acid-free paper.

About the Authors

Dr. Stephen G. Payne is an ex-CEO intent on helping leaders from all walks of life achieve their greatest potential for growth. For 14 years, he has brought his readily doable approach to performance acceleration to CEOs and senior executives, to groups of aspiring leaders, and to MBA students. A crisp focus on the situation through 1-Paging is, in Stephen's view, a critical tool for any leader's journey.

Alan S. W. Dowie is a senior manager with a leading global healthcare company. For more than a decade, Alan has been an enthusiastic exponent of 1-Paging, applying this focused way of thinking and acting to local and international business situations. He has found 1-Paging to be a powerful way to achieve goals by galvanizing diverse groups, regardless of functional and geographic barriers.

Stephen and Alan combine to be the voice of the busy senior manager who narrates this book.

Download their 1-Paging templates, build your own game plan, and share with other users at:

Manage Your World

On

ONE PAGE

Contents

1-Paging [wun pājing] *n./v.*

1. Focusing your intentions succinctly onto 1-Page.

2. Communicating your 1-Page plan confidently to get rapid alignment with your team.

3. Renewing your 1-Page plan constantly through five key questions that keep your focus sharp.

4. Executing your 1-Page plan, reporting progress, and running meetings with the same disciplined focus.

There are boxes like the one below throughout this book. Each applies the concept of 1-Paging by distilling key information onto a single page. This first one distills the entire book.

1-Paging This Entire Book

- *It's all about a simple idea that can substantially improve your results. Express your plan on a single page.* **1-Page it!** *The clarity and focus you get will boost your confidence, plus you will be holding a great tool for communicating with your team.*

- *1-Paging is the work you do to set out and keep your situation clearly stated on one page. Think of it as answering powerful questions that deliver a crisp mental focus on what you need to get done. Then, whenever distractions try to derail you, you stay on track by repeating the questions.*

- *This book helps you discover the benefits of 1-Paging through a remarkable tool called the 1-Page Game Plan. It is a multipurpose 1-Paging template you use to build a crystal-clear action plan to keep you and your team focused on delivering your goals.*

- *1-Paging with the 1-Page Game Plan really works! It has already delivered great results for 1-Paging users in a wide range of situations. Some of them have generously contributed their experiences by writing the 1-Paging in Action reports in this book.*

- *To see more, to download the 1-Page Game Plan templates, or to share your 1-Paging with other users, go to:*

1-Paging.com

Throughout the book you will see 1-Paging in Action reports like the one below. Each one is someone's real world experience of 1-Paging.

1-Paging in Action

By David O'Keeffe
General Manager
Bard Ltd.

Issue:
Having recently created a new countrywide sales team, it was critical to provide clarity on what we were trying to achieve and how we were going to drive the business forward. It was essential to keep my team focused on value-creating activities and to achieve their buy-in.

Before:
Generally, we did a good job of communicating in meetings, presentations and networking within the organization. It proved difficult to maintain focus because we lacked a simple way to state, in a clear objective manner, what we were trying to achieve and how all stakeholders could help us achieve our growth goals and projects.

1-Paging:
Our 1-Pager was created in a workshop approach with my direct reports. This created strong buy-in to the overall process from my team and made it much easier for them to cascade the 1-Pager down the entire organization. There was a great sense of relief and optimism when we collectively realized that the complex and previously daunting task of building a country organization could be encapsulated in 1-Page of key strategies, goals, measures, and actions.

After:
Our growth results have been remarkable. Not only do we complete our 1-Paging at the country level but each individual territory has a 1-Page Game Plan that is totally aligned with the country goals and strategies. Now all team members know exactly what they have to achieve and how their individual goals drive the country-level growth. Our 1-Pager is always at hand to maintain daily focus. We would never have got this level of clarity by the traditional strategic planning process.

The 1-Page Game Plan uses symbols to distill elements of your world onto one page. Make a mental note of these great focusing questions and their game plan symbols.

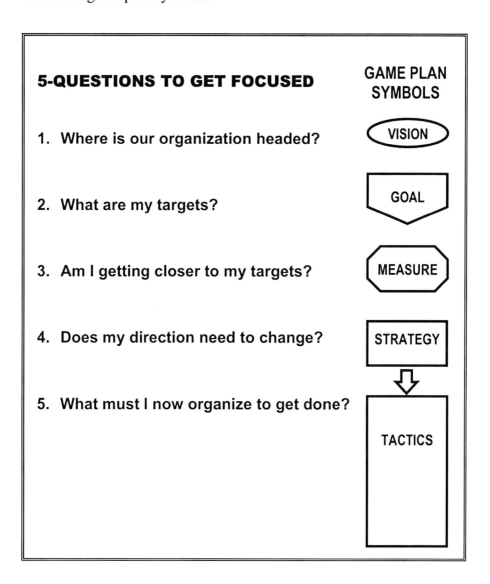

1-Paging Chapter One

- *Outstanding individual and team performance stem from focusing hearts, minds, and actions on the <u>vital few</u> things that deliver growth.*

- *Discovering the <u>vital few</u> is the hard work we call focusing. To maintain the greatest focus, apply the 5-Questions of 1-Paging to your situation:*

  1. *Where is our organization headed, and what are the top-level priorities?*
  2. *What are my (or my team's) growth targets or goals, and can I see their linkage to the organizational priorities?*
  3. *Am I getting closer to my targets, and can I see my performance gap clearly whenever I need to look?*
  4. *Does my direction need to change due to internal and external forces impacting me since I last looked?*
  5. *Right now, what must I organize to get done in order to meet my (or my team's) goals?*

- *By answering these 5-Questions, your alignment to your goals is boosted. If you also try to distill your answers onto 1-Page, this focusing effect becomes turbocharged—especially in a group setting.*

- *The 1-Page Game Plan is a great tool for individual and group 1-Paging. It is simple to use, it fits any situation or project, and it transforms the <u>vital few</u> things into a clear, renewable, action plan.*

CHAPTER ONE

Starting 1-Paging

Losing focus is a modern-day epidemic. We get so crammed with information and tasks that we lose sight of where we are trying to go. As a simple self-evaluation, think about your job or current situation and ask yourself these questions:

> *Am I certain that <u>all</u> my busy activities today are really necessary to achieving my goals? What about yesterday?*

> *Am I too often triggered into action by disruptions that lead me nowhere?*

> *Are my days so over-piled with stuff that the pleasure of <u>real</u> achievement seems to elude me?*

Be honest, do these questions raise any doubts about how well you stay focused as you manage your world?

Let me introduce myself. I'm a busy senior manager who has to keep his organization focused on achieving important targets—despite all the constant interruptions and disruptions. I should also tell you that I'm a passionate believer in the whole idea of 1-Paging. Why? Because, thankfully, I've seen all the positive changes that have happened since we got focused by 1-Paging.

Before my 1-Paging days, despite a good start to things, the dreaded distraction demon always crept up and took us off track. We operated as though doing <u>more</u> work was actually getting the <u>right</u> work done, as though being very active meant we were on the right track. In reality, we were mostly far off track and not seeing the way back. We were too busy working hard. What a waste!

Have you experienced this problem of being pulled off track by endless disruptions? With such rapid communications these days, it can become an overwhelming force. When I look around, I see the same problem frustrating so many people in both their professional and private lives. Just what do we have to do to feel consistently aligned?

Imagine how confidence-boosting it would be to be able to state every day: "I'm clear about the <u>critical few</u> things I need to focus on and where successful completion of them will get me."

Or, on the much grander scale of a large organization, imagine being able to say this:

"In our organization, we have a clear, shared understanding of where we are headed—backed up by consistency of approach. If our CEO leaves tomorrow, we know his successor will not tear apart the organization and start again. There's a consistency of message. If you go anywhere and speak to anyone, they can explain concisely <u>what's really important around here</u>. Our professional and personal goals are aligned, that's why we share a sense of productivity as we work alongside each other."

Are these pipe dreams? Since I've become a user of 1-Paging and seen the improvements we have achieved, I can tell you that they are not. 1-Paging is a simple idea with a big result. It keeps me and my team on the track that leads to performance.

But please don't just take my word for it. Many users of 1-Paging have had the same positive, "now I get how to stay focused" experience. They too stay focused on doing the right things thanks to 1-Paging. With the help of some of them, plus the 1-Paging.com website, my mission here is to help you discover how 1-Paging can do the same for you.

Adopt 1-Paging as your personal focusing device for the distracting times ahead. It really helps you get the right things done.

Problem Clarification

It's not simply hour-by-hour, or day-by-day, interruptions that push you and me off track as we try to achieve our plans, or even that we get deflected by better ideas of what we should be doing. It's the fact that we can't easily tell whether each interruption or better idea is the right one to follow. The apparently straightforward connection between the action and successful result gets unbelievably confused these days—so much so that the default can quickly become either doing nothing or trying to do everything. Can you relate to this problem? I know it all too well.

In a large organization, you can see how this confusion gets amplified. In the absence of clear direction, groups of people function like disconnected spinning cogs. From your own cog, it seems virtually impossible to know whether the cogs are connected in any coherent way. Even well-crafted and very well-intentioned communications  end up gumming up, rather than lubricating, the machine.

Whatever happened to the brilliant idea that the computer age was supposed to offer increased efficiency, communication, and relaxation time for us all? It certainly fooled me—and my family. The norm these days is to have loads of new and "better" initiatives, meeting mania, and dozens of "urgent" e-mails piling up each day. How can I give my team the best direction, support, and motivation if I'm unclear about my own priorities for action? As I jokingly say to my team, "How many <u>top</u> priorities does it take to get <u>complete</u> chaos?"

Of course, I could declare that my team "just doesn't get it" and look for "better" people, but, in reality, their confusion is the same as mine and, come to think of it, my boss's. It's so easy for any of us to lose sight of the winning post these days.

I have also noticed that I, and so many other people I see, let our frustrations with "I'm so busy" rule our lives. We blame "them" for our "intense schedules," our "inability to get anything accomplished," and, even worse, we blame "them" that life's satisfaction and plain old fun are less apparent.

Question: Why is it that losing sight of what it takes to be successful causes so much discomfort?

Answer: Life, at home and work, is becoming far more complicated to organize. The old reliable structures are gone, replaced by shifting, more changeable arrangements. In all these new patterns, we get confused, and then negative emotions emerge. This feeling-trapped sensation, without a clear target and a way out, is very uncomfortable. Wanting relief becomes a central issue in our lives.

Result: Loss of personal focus, poor performance, fatigue, lowered team morale, and ineffective leadership.

Enough about the problem! How do we improve these unfocused and frustrating situations with 1-Paging?

My Simple Principle

The problem is certainly not solved with more complexity. More of the same only adds to the frustration. It needs something simple. Here is the **nugget**, the core principle, behind 1-Paging:

> *To prevent confusion in our fast-moving, matrix-managed world, get back to <u>basic</u> management practices.*

In other words, stick to the basics. I mean things like meeting people face-to-face, giving simple, clear directions, and providing honest feedback. Doing this is even more important in today's fast-paced world, but somehow, in all our rushing around, we tend to skip it. Yet, as things get more complex and uncertain, simple and clear management methods are really all we need to keep us balanced.

Questions That Focus

I never enter a complex situation without this principle. The more mind-bogglingly difficult the topic, the simpler I try to manage it.

Here is how I use it to defeat the distraction demon. From a professional point of view (Note: Applying this from a personal growth point of view is in Chapter 6), in order to stay on track, we simply need to answer this sequence of 5-Questions:

1. *Where is our organization headed, and what are the top-level priorities?*

2. *What are my (or my team's) targets or goals, and can I see the linkage to the bigger organizational priorities?*

3. *Am I getting closer to my targets, and can I see my performance gap clearly whenever I need to look?*

4. *Does my direction need to change because internal and external forces have impacted me recently?*

5. *Right now, what must I organize to get done in order to meet my (or my team's) goals?*

Picture your job, or one of your important projects, and try asking and answering these five questions in sequence. The elements you need to stay focused will start to emerge. This is not rocket science; it's just basic management stuff that I never used to start with, let alone practiced regularly. Why not? you may well ask.

Frankly, I am at the heart of the issue rather than my work situation. All too often I would overcomplicate things by diving in and doing, rather than thinking. Call it my lack of courage, determination, or whatever you like, but if I am unwilling to confront these basic questions of focusing for me or my team, then who will? Nobody. Ask yourself the same question.

Joined-Up Thinking

Applying the simple flow of the 5-Questions got me thinking clearly about how we fit into the overall company plan. My breakthrough moment occurred when I realized that there was no single place to go to see all the key activities that emerge as answers.

So I set about gathering the information from various sources and, armed with my principle of simplicity, decided to try 1-Paging— focusing my answers onto a single page. It was far from perfect the first time, but the energy of just getting moving, focusing, and sharing the results can be contagious.

My colleagues' responses helped me enormously. The 5-Questions and my tentative 1-Paging seemed to boost their focus, too. They quickly grasped the value of the 1-Page representation and added their improvements. Once we had a working version at the top level, they started to create their individual, complementary 1-Page picture. Before we knew it, 1-Pagers started to appear at meetings, with small enhancements being added. It actually became quite competitive, but in a positive way, as we shared improvements to the process.

To my surprise, a 1-Paging movement had started. By keeping things simple and writing the answers on a single page, we could see, communicate, and remember what needed to be done. It was a transferable technique my team could understand, and it felt great— like I had recovered some lost leadership power.

One <u>vital</u> element emerged very quickly. It's perilous to skip the fourth question: *Does my direction need to change because internal and external forces have impacted me recently?* This question points to what was causing our loss of focus. Without thinking through the answer, we were lulled into the false belief that we were on track to achieve our goals when, in reality, conditions had changed, and we were off track. It's called the **Renewal Question** because asking and answering it <u>repeatedly</u> spurs us to think about whether our plans need to change, which in turn helps us stay on track. If, like me, you ever worked madly to complete something that led nowhere, then you experienced firsthand the frustration of omitting the renewal question. These days, my thinking is characterized by more initiative and a willingness to repeat the 5-Questions with extra emphasis on the renewal question. Think of them as weapons that slay the distraction demon.

Also, it's self-evident that this repeating the questions is so much easier when there is just one page of information to deal with. It's simple management again.

The Alignment Experience

Aligned is what I call the mental state we all get to when we complete our 1-Paging together. Other users use phrases like "connected," "in-step," and "pulling together." When I'm feeling aligned after 1-Paging, I am focused, clearer, calmer, and more productive. I'm better able to think problems through with my team. I don't overreact to events, and I'm able to plan ahead without too much worrying. At a gut level I sense we're on track.

The alignment feelings of my team members are absolutely critical to me. My team leadership nugget on this topic is:

> *Take <u>personal ownership</u> of the individual and collective alignment of your team, and you will control your destiny.*

Do you get the impression that I believe misalignment of me and my team is my problem and not someone else's? It's true. It's my job to make sure that my people keep a tangible sense of the right thing to do. Once they have it, they can draw on it whenever conditions change, especially when I'm not around.

By the way, when I say "aligning my people," I'm referring to individuals who may be located in different departments, countries, or even continents. The consequences of failing to keep them in the picture can be dire—including their deciding to go elsewhere for job satisfaction.

When I worked in a multinational organization, we used the aligning power of 1-Paging across the entire globe. Initially, we all found it hard to communicate on an international basis. The senior leaders were frustrated at the apparent lack of local understanding or acceptance of what they were trying to do. A situation of "us and them" was emerging. 1-Paging came to the rescue.

The turning point came when I persuaded senior management to craft their management board 1-Pager. I didn't begin by telling them about 1-Paging; I simply got them to have a structured conversation about their future picture of the company using the 5-Questions. Armed with the information from the meeting, I prepared and duly presented it to them in the well-organized 1-Paging format you will be seeing soon. Viewing their ideas on a single page was a tremendous tonic. Before too long, each board member used the 5-Questions to create his or her own 1-Pager to support the top-level one. Each one rapidly cascaded that picture as a communication and planning tool for his or her staff in our global locations. Now, everyone could begin to see quite simply what the company was trying to do. This sparked teams at local sites into action, preparing and communicating their 1-Pagers to align with the higher-level picture. Soon afterward they started using it to measure progress and run meetings. It rapidly became "the way we work around the world."

If you are in a similar situation, here is the nugget on this topic:

> *When using 1-Paging to align a group or team, start with the 5-Questions, not the 1-Page format. It's the questions that create focus; the information you gather can always be expressed in a 1-Pager format when you follow up.*

The Flexible Aligning Tool

Building and sustaining alignment with the 5-Questions is accelerated when you use the remarkable **1-Page Game Plan** (Note: From here I'll often simply call it the **1-Pager**.) True to my management philosophy, it is nothing more than a simple template with all the elements of a plan in a clear picture that can be shared and updated easily.

Here is the blank layout as it prints on a single page. It has 5 levels, corresponding to the 5-Questions: **Vision** at the top, then my **Goals**, with **Measures**, **Strategies**, and **Tactics** downward under each goal.

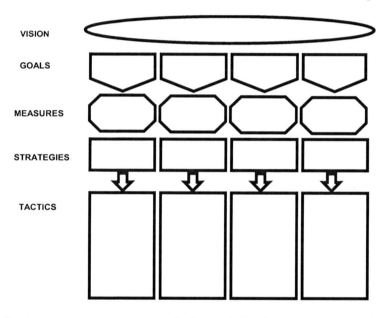

It really has answered my need for a 1-Paging process, a simple process, to keep me and my team fully aligned with our goals in the face of so many distractions.

Familiarize yourself with the different shapes, because my purpose now is to get you started by showing you how my 1-Pager is built.

1-Paging Advice: Chapter 1

- If you're spending more time figuring out where you are going than leading your team to get there—STOP. You are already in the wrong place. Practice 1-Paging your situation with the 5-Questions in any format that works for you.

- If you start telling others that your people just don't get it, you are again in the wrong place. You must own <u>their</u> experience of <u>their</u> alignment to your targets, not your experience of their misalignment. If you're not conscious of your attitude toward their alignment, start immediately discussing it with them. How? Just ask them to complete the 5-Questions.

- Don't give up on the power of simple management practices like meeting face-to-face, asking and answering honest, basic questions, setting clear direction using 1-Paging, and giving good feedback. If you are a manager, this will always be 90 percent of your job.

- Never imagine that you will need to answer the 5-Questions only once. It's less of an event, and more of a process of constant renewal. That means learning how to constantly adapt the questions to your situation. Expect to create a unique approach to 1-Paging.

- When it comes to aligning a complex team such as one geographically or functionally spread, it is safe to assume, first, that out of sight is indeed out of mind, and, second, that it's <u>your</u> problem. Acceptance of this fact is the gateway to exceptional results from using the 5-Questions and the 1-Page Game Plan.

1-Paging in Action

By Terry Herring
President
inVentiv Commercial Services

Issue:

inVentiv Commercial Services is a pharmaceutical sales, compliance, and marketing company. In 2002, as the newly appointed president, I was given the opportunity, with a team of very talented people, to return the business to profitability.

Before:

Typical of a turnaround situation, many of the senior executives in the business had left, there was low morale, our good people were leaving, and communication with our employees was breaking down. Quickly, we focused on: finding and grooming the right people, enhancing our communication, creating and establishing support for a succinct 1-Page planning process, identifying key operating principles for all employees, and providing incentives for superior performance.

1-Paging:

From the top-level 1-Pager we cascaded down one organizational level, ensuring the same goal structure at the top of each plan: a) revenue goal, b) earnings goal, c) efficiencies and process management, d) new product and business development, and e) development of people. We added some basic but invaluable operating principles like: find solutions not issues, be personally accountable for your results, and recognize others and their accomplishments.

After:

In five short years, our stock price has grown from approximately $1 to over $30, with revenue from this core business unit doubling, and earnings increasing from breakeven to $50 million. We have also had the great pleasure of being recognized in the business community for our success. The 1-Page Game Plan is now fully institutionalized into the month-by-month management process and the annual business planning cycle. The organizational focus 1-Paging creates is essential to sustaining our growth.

1-Paging Chapter Two

■ *The 1-Page Game Plan is an explicit, written version of your entire Vision—what an individual or team has to do to be successful. It communicates the Vision Statement, Goals, Measures, Strategies, and Tactics in a format that follows the 5-Questions.*

■ *At the top of the One-Page Game Plan, the <u>Vision Statement</u> changes only very occasionally. It is a phrase you use to inspire and refresh the sense of greater possibility in you and your team members.*

■ *The <u>Goals</u> come below the Vision Statement:*

  • *An <u>Accountability Goal</u> is a written statement of a target that the team must achieve by a given date; it <u>always</u> needs to be clear, observable and, ideally, measurable.*

  • *A <u>Relationship Goal</u> sets out a desired impact on people and their attitudes. These Goals are often not directly measurable, but that's not a problem.*

■ *Beyond three of four goals, most teams struggle to stay focused—the burden of staying aligned exceeds the burden of execution. <u>Great</u> goals are few in number and expressed so crisply that they flow comfortably through the minds of people in the organization.*

CHAPTER TWO

Vision and Goals

The effectiveness of 1-Paging improves dramatically when you adopt the elementary symbols of the 1-Page Game Plan. It is a template of five layers into which we type words—the answers to the 5-Questions. In the next few chapters, using my team's plan as a model, you will see the symbols in each layer in the sequence you need to build your own 1-Pager.

1-PAGING SYMBOLS

We start at the top two layers, keeping our principle of simplicity close at hand.

A **Vision** is a critical element in creating something new. It is an image of the thing we want that is yet to come into existence—like my mental picture of becoming a senior executive running our new plant, or the architect's drawing of the new plant yet to be built. One version of my vision may be spoken or written down, while another version exists in my mind— that's the translation of the written or spoken words into my own feelings and expectations regarding the future.

Think of this latter version as a <u>powerful mental picture</u> that energizes and keeps me on track as I work, especially when the distraction demon is about. Creating and sustaining the power of this picture in me and my team is the entire purpose of our 1-Paging work.

Organizations and teams have visions, too. They are written or visual images of the hoped-for things that will achieve greater performance for everyone. Often they contain punchy phrases like "We will Be

Number One in Our Industry," or "We're the Top Quality Service Company." Often, they are accompanied by detailed plans of how to get there. They're all very good but seldom do they instantly connect to that powerful energizing place in people's minds.

If you think of a team as a collection of distinct individual minds, often with very different backgrounds and expectations, you can see that the way each person relates to future success or growth becomes critically important to the shared focus of the whole team. A good vision serves to mentally energize an individual performance in the context of the overall group's goal, just like the players in a football team are motivated to play their best to get the winning score.

Try picturing a game of football where the scoring, goal posts, teams, and markings on the field are constantly changing! In many organizations that's what rapid change feels like. Without anticipating the effect this shifting has on people, you can end up, as I used to, unwittingly motivating good people without getting to the right result. "Great team effort everyone, great score, wrong game—sorry, but we all just lost!"

Here are the nuggets on vision:

> *Use the 1-Page Game Plan format to 1-Page your vision of what has to be achieved, how you have to achieve it, and how you will measure progress.*

> *Use it repeatedly to energize people's performance, including your own, as you ask and answer the 5-Questions layer by layer.*

Having seen tremendous benefit from broad use of the 1-Pager, I am confident that it is flexible enough for any project, team, or structure.

Vision Statement (Question 1: Where are we headed?)

A **Vision Statement** is just one element of a vision and, therefore, one part of a 1-Page Game Plan. It is a written, inspirational phrase that guides the sense of possibility for the team. Here are some real-world examples:

> "We are the pioneers of new technologies for Internet searching."

> "We are the results-focused marketing team driving new growth in all segments."

> "Our group is dedicated to providing each patient and family with an outstanding experience of high quality healthcare."

Some leaders see these vision statements as a waste of time. I disagree. They miss the value that a vision statement brings by not only expressing "what we want to achieve" but also capturing the essence of "what we are all about becoming" as we work together. This shared sense of belonging to a project is really valuable.

Here's the nugget on a vision statement for your 1-Paging:

> *Create a short vision statement for you or your team and use it to inspire the sense of greater possibility.*

The Team With Superior Execution, Customer Penetration, and Profitable Growth

The vision statement goes at the top layer of the 1-Pager. Above is ours as I typed it into the template. If you lead a team, try to create a vision statement early on that really connects people at the gut level.

Later on, when the team is facing obstacles to executing the plan, you will see its alignment pay off.

Question: After the vision statement, what else would you expect to see on your team's 1-Pager?

Answer: The details of what you need to do to be successful—your plan—organized concisely to help you stay aligned and energized, and to help you periodically ask and answer the 5-Questions.

Result: A plan that stays alive in people's minds because you can easily share it and even update it in real-time via laptop and projector.

Setting Clear Goals (Question 2: What are my targets?)

The next layer on the 1-Pager template is where you describe your **Goals**, the things you have to deliver. True to form, I have three simple rules. First, a goal should be a clear statement of the outcomes we need to achieve within a time-bound period. Second, each goal should be constructed so that we can measure whether or not we are on track. Third, and my favorite, the fewer we have the better.

I always start with **Accountability Goals** that state the specific results we expect to achieve in measurable terms. On the template, they look like the one above.

Can you create such a crisp accountability goal that fits your job or project situation? Ask yourself: What do I have to <u>produce</u> this month, or week?

Another example of an accountability goal:

As you memorize the shape of the goal box on the template, notice that both these accountability goals express a clear growth target in time which can be measured.

However, this does not imply that <u>all</u> goals are necessarily numbers driven. Non-measurable goals are usually those that impact the changing of people's attitudes and abilities.

These are called **Relationship Goals**. They express the growth we need in attitudes and competence in order to enable great performance by the team, as well as others who influence the team, like our colleagues across our worldwide organization who work with us.

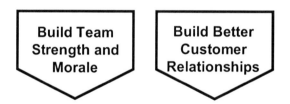

Can you think of your primary relationship goal?

(Note: The templates at www.1-Paging.com use color as well as shading.)

Sharing the Goal Setting

As I mentioned earlier, I've learned that the best team alignment is achieved when my team members develop their own 1-Pagers with their teams just as they do with me. It's both a top-down and a bottom-up process. (Note: Much more on this process is covered in Chapter 5.)

Here is how it works: We come together and distill things down to the critical few accountability and relationship goals for growth using the 5-Questions. Then we meet regularly, include our partners in other departments, and keep the plan up-to-date. It's simple management, yet again.

I like to picture everyone associated with my team across the entire organization as clearly understanding their critical few accountability and relationship goals that they have to achieve for the success of us all. Like an elastic spider's web of clear 1-Pagers that link to our top-level targets. When adverse things happen, as they often do, we stay flexibly connected. The powerful bond of our shared sense of alignment and clarity is a mighty defense against the distraction demon.

Back to the process of building a 1-Pager.

The top two layers of my 1-Pager are completed by adding the remaining goals to the template. It now looks like this:

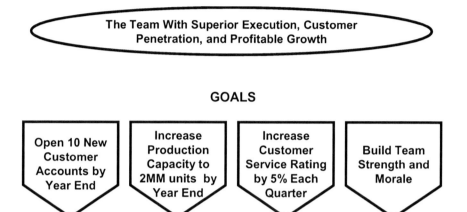

VISION STATEMENT

The Team With Superior Execution, Customer Penetration, and Profitable Growth

GOALS

Open 10 New Customer Accounts by Year End

Increase Production Capacity to 2MM units by Year End

Increase Customer Service Rating by 5% Each Quarter

Build Team Strength and Morale

It takes practice to whittle goals down to the critical few. Can you write your three or four? On a single sheet?

I should point out that for any given job or project, the vision statement at the top does not change. The accountability and relationship goals might change, though not frequently. (Note: You will see later that the strategies and tactics below each goal do change as we use the 5-Questions and work is accomplished.)

Question: Having placed your goals onto the template, should you now move down to defining strategies and tactics to achieve these goals?

Answer: Absolutely not! If you can't measure it, it's not yet a great goal.

So let's pause to get more 1-Paging advice on vision and goals and then move quickly down to the measures layer of the 1-Pager.

1-Paging Advice: Chapter Two

- The test of a good written vision statement is its ability to inspire and motivate your team, not the political correctness of the language. Let your team express things that bind them together in their own unique way.

- Vision statement and goal development should usually be done as a team activity. There are two exceptions—when the team is new to the 1-Paging process, and when a directed management style is more appropriate.

- Beware of causing confusion if you cascade goals throughout your organization. Here's a tip: Start by cascading one level down and across only. Be sure to find sufficient time and involve the right people in the process.

- Install your system of measuring weekly or monthly progress before defining how you will achieve your goal. This is a vital sanity check on your accountability and relationship goals. If you find yourself struggling to find ways to measure the gap, loop back and redefine your goals with even more clarity.

1-Paging in Action

By Peter Gray
Chief Executive Officer
ICON plc

Issue:
The company was growing fast, and it needed to transition from being opportunistic and reactive to being professional and strategic, while avoiding bureaucracy and retaining the flexibility and focus that had been the source of our success.

Before:
Targets were based on a one-year budget and the focus was on the next quarter. As we grew, different divisions, regions, and departments were developing their own solutions to common problems, leading to divergence of approach, and where problems were not common, they were developing solutions that worked for them, but did not consider the broader needs of the company.

1-Paging:
We created a simple, 1-Page "3-year goal map" for the company. We identified what we believed our needed core competencies were and set about building them in. We prioritized all the initiatives that were being pursued for the organization, ensured they were shared, and assigned "owners" to progress them and report on the dashboard. We then had departments prepare their own 1-Pagers looking just 1-year ahead. Through this process we identified misalignments between departments and divisions and worked together to realign them.

After:
We got great feedback across the organization that, for the first time, there was a clear vision of where we were going and what we were trying to be. Because people could see our company dashboard, we got better collaboration across the organization and buy-in to initiatives that previously would have been seen as infringing on the independence of divisions. These days I see department and individual 1-Pagers throughout the entire organization.

1-Paging Chapter Three

■ *Think of your goals and their measures as tightly bound together—they can never be apart. If you can't measure your progress toward an accountability goal then surely your goal is not adequately expressed as an outcome. This is a <u>critical</u> rule.*

■ *Some goals are hard to measure, very often those that have to do with people, but even these goals can be clear and have sufficient sub-elements of measurement so they are not simply pie-in-the-sky.*

■ *Creating a measurement system should always start before building strategies and tactics. If you can't measure goals clearly, look for what you can do instead. Can you visualize "right activity" at some point in the process? If so, that can be the basis of discovering a surrogate measure.*

■ *Visually attractive dashboards are the key to alignment when the team meets. Clear minds need simple dashboards to stay on track and focus on where to take corrective action. Look for simple pictorial representation. Don't rush to implementation without one.*

CHAPTER THREE

Measures Before Action

It's an obvious, yet often ignored, fact that unless we can track our progress in achieving a goal, we can't see if we are getting closer to achieving it. The performance gap—between where we are today and our future goal—is always easy to see at the start, but it's another thing altogether to regularly **measure** the gap along the way. Yet how else can our day-by-day work be focused on getting the gap closed?

1-PAGING SYMBOL

MEASURE

This simple 1-Paging discipline of creating and tracking measures scares some people away from accountability for their goals. They say things like, "Nice picture and logical too, but won't all this discipline act as a barrier to innovation and creativity?" Then they either resist the process or, even worse, they support 1-Paging in principle then completely ignore it in practice and drift off track.

I beg to differ. In my experience, the crisp alignment we get with our 1-Paging makes it the perfect vehicle to ensure that our creative activities are translated into <u>real</u> deliverables. Without the discipline of measuring my progress creativity remains far too conceptual. Would you expect your car to create its own roads? Of course not. Instead you create an excellent journey for yourself by choosing from a wide selection of destinations and vehicles by sticking to the existing roads—provided you know where you are trying to get to (goal), by when you need to get there (goal), and how far you have come (measure).

Beware of the Fuzziness Demon

We all have to guard against creating 1-Pager goals that are vague and fuzzy, and therefore cannot be measured. Look at these examples:

Coordinate the Network of Customer Partners

Improve Our Position in the Market

Work Much Harder Than Last Year!

Ask yourself just what and how often you would measure them to know how well you are on track and closing the performance gap. Your answers will be fuzzy.

Fuzzy goals like these run the risk of never being achieved because nobody can tell if or when the needed outcome is achieved. The distraction demon's twin brother, the fuzziness demon, wants you to be unclear, de-motivated, and waste people's time, energy, and money.

Don't confuse fuzziness—mental vagueness of purpose—with complexity. You can do the work of getting clear in the most complex situations, if you choose. And remember the enemy of the fuzziness demon is the 1-Paging user who is committed to regularly asking the 5-Questions that build clarity and alignment.

The hard truth is this: To stay focused on achieving performance, you have to learn to express even the most amorphous goals in terms of tangible outcomes and measures so that your team, your colleagues, and your boss can be clear on what you are all achieving for your organization.

There can be no hiding from accountability. Every successful leader has learned to fight fuzziness in all its manifest forms. Try to think of the 5-Questions and the 1-Pager as essential weapons in your fuzziness fighting force.

Measurement (Question 3: Am I getting closer to my targets?)

If you build accountability goals with clear deliverables and time scales, they are far from fuzzy, and therefore the measurement of the performance gap over time becomes quite straightforward.

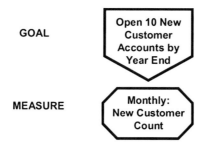

Note the eight-sided symbol we type in for a measure. It is under the goal as we work down the 1-Pager.

Remember, at this stage of building my plan, I am not trying to describe <u>how</u> we will achieve the accountability goal. That comes later when we define strategies and tactics. At this stage, we simply need to be certain that we have a goal with a clear measure and frequency of measurement.

Often, if you can't find a clear measurement for an accountability goal, the chances are there's something wrong with the goal. It's best to go back and work at restating it in a less fuzzy way.

Measuring Relationship Goals

How do we find measures and track progress for the less tangible relationship goals? They have a degree of built-in fuzziness already.

Fortunately, I have my Six Sigma training to help me answer this question. Six Sigma taught me to first define the goal, and then discover and measure the **critical-to-quality** elements required to achieve the goal. I can gather data or use experience to discover what these critical-to-quality elements will be. Then I can find a method of measuring performance of these elements instead of my relationship goal. It's not perfect but it's the best alternative I've found.

For example, I had a relationship goal to develop more leaders in our organization by offering broader work experience. Analysis of the problem yielded a number of critical-to-quality factors—the track records of people, their aptitude to take on new roles, and the strength of successors available to backfill. I chose to measure progress by tracking the strength and performance of successors.

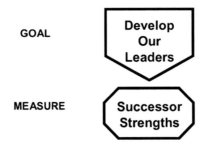

Here's another example: Imagine you and I have a relationship goal to attract better people to our organization. There are many critical-to-quality factors here—finding the right candidates, the interview selection process, the way we train and induct new people, and so on. Further analysis yields a simple fact: If you don't have better candidates, you don't recruit better people. Now the track record, diversity, and experience level of our candidates is something we can try to quantify.

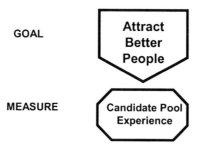

Again, it's not perfect, but it helps reduce fuzziness and give a measure of our progress with a higher level of confidence.

Goal measurement goes far beyond the scope of 1-Paging. Should you need them, search and you will discover many sophisticated methods, including surveys of customers, owners, suppliers, and employees. Just don't forget my first nugget of keeping to simple basics.

Creating a Simple Dashboard

Whenever I take measures of my goals, I display the result on my **Dashboard**—a set of clear indicators of the gap between where we are and where we need to get to. The purpose of the dashboard is to support the 5-Questions improvement process by provides <u>accurate</u> progress data in a <u>visually attractive format</u> that brings attention to where effort is needed. Dashboards can come in many shapes and sizes. But take care: Sometimes they take on a life of their own and require an army of people to administer them.

True to form, the nugget on dashboards is simple:

> *Make your dashboard easy to understand, maintain, and update, but, above all, make it show where <u>action</u> is needed.*

So build your dashboard before you start your journey!

To illustrate how to build a dashboard, here is my 1-Pager with the measurement layer completed under the goals.

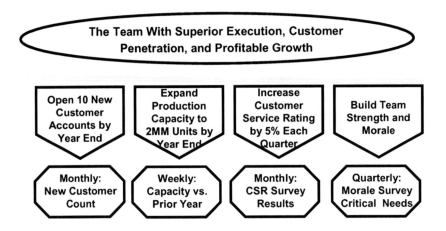

I keep the dashboard on a separate page or screen from my 1-Pager. It needs to show my progress by answering basic questions about my job or project. For my accountability and relationship goals, these are questions like: "Did we reach our new customer count target this month?" or "How much production capacity do we have available for next month?" or "Is the morale of our organization improving?"

On my 1-Pager, above, imagine a row of lights under each goal. (Note: Again, the downloads at www.1-Paging.com use color.)

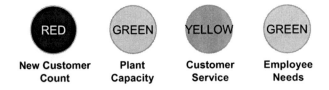

The colors tell me where we have a performance gap in achieving our goal—red for problem in closing the performance gap, yellow when

I'm cautious, and green when things are going well. This is my top-level dashboard. It's pointing to where we need to dig in further to look at our activities. Imagine clicking on any one of the lights to see where I need more attention

I always choose this simple format that both aligns with the 1-Pager and gets our attention.

Clicking on the red light for New Customer Count might produce the following sub-dashboard for further examination.

	Plan	Revised Plan	Status
Goal: Open 10 New Customer Accounts by Year End	December		
Measure: Monthly Customer Count			YELLOW
Critical-to-Quality			
- Rebuild Trade Show Stand	April		Green
- Install Contact Database System	February		Green
- Review and Follow Up Old Contact List	March		Green
- Expand Trade Show Sales Team	June	August	RED

Legend		
Minimal risk to meet 1-Pager commitments.	Green
Moderate risk, yet within range. Action planned.	YELLOW
Significantly off track. Critical Issue. Action required.	RED

In my experience, the measures with greatest impact are often in the area least prone to measurement. For example, when I was 1-Paging a sales-force improvement project, I discovered that my sales colleagues saw their selling as an "art" that could not be broken down into specific strategies, tactics, and measures. They argued that such a structuring would interfere with their pursuit of results. However, by analyzing their specific work habits, I showed them what the cause and effect of certain activities, such as frequency of customer contact, was having on their sales performance dashboard.

Since the idea captured their imagination, they adopted it with gusto, proudly using their dashboards to show how systematic deployment of their individual 1-Pager was improving their dashboard scores. The focus, energy, and enthusiasm with which they embraced the 1-Pager has been one of the most rewarding moments on my entire 1-Paging journey. Many of those colleagues moved to senior positions in our company and they continue to be 1-Paging "evangelists" to this day.

Here is the underlying nugget they uncovered:

> *The process of 1-Paging not only helps you focus on what delivers results; it also neatly exposes the areas you <u>don't</u> need to work on, i.e., where you are wasting time and energy with no impact on your dashboard.*

When you try creating the measures and dashboard for your goals, expect that it will take a few iterations before the right set of measures is found. Try to take a critical view of whether your activities are really delivering results you can measure. Avoid the fuzziness demon at all costs.

Let's review the 1-Paging advice on this topic and move on to the remaining elements of the 1-Page Game Plan.

1-Paging Advice: Chapter Three

- Rushing toward achieving goals without knowing measures causes confusion and lowers team morale—not in the initial stages of team working when team spirits are high, but during the subsequent ups and downs when, quite literally, you can't see where you are.

- It's often easier to come up with multiple progress measures for the same goal. The important work is distilling them down to the critical few dashboard measures that truly show progress toward the goal. Your purpose is to achieve the goals, not to operate a dashboard like a jet aircraft.

- Completion of some step in your plan is not a measure of goal achievement. The measure is the downstream impact achieved as a <u>result</u> of your completed task. If you find yourself believing otherwise by saying things like: "We must be getting closer to the target because we've finished our tasks," then your goal may not be clear and measurable—the fuzziness demon is running your team.

- Visually attractive dashboards are important to team alignment. Don't rush to implementation without one. To evolve to the best dashboard, continually ask the 5-Questions and look for the simplest pictorial representation. Simple color schemes that represent the performance gap are usually sufficient. Be imaginative!

1-Paging in Action

By Bill Cordivari
Former President
Ortho Dermatological (J&J)

Issue:
I inherited a terrible business situation where the team was overwhelmed by a well-publicized legal crisis. Growth was flat, and there was a leadership void as well as plummeting morale.

Before:
Survival cliques had formed. Everybody was doing their own thing. Common-sense business disciplines had broken down. For example, people launched projects spending someone else's budget moneys and assuming no accountability for the outcome. The future was bleak.

1-Paging:
Using a 1-Pager, we captured our vision (where we wanted to go and what we wanted to become) and our mission (why we existed and the purpose of our organization.) Our dashboard showed our current year and five-year financial goals to help us balance short- and longer-term thinking. We prioritized all key activities and projects under five top-level goals; things like: expand market share of core business, in-license new products, and develop and get people promoted. We had clear owner-drivers for each goal. We opened all team meetings with the 1-Pager, plus I used it in most one-on-one discussions about the business.

After:
The majority of the team coalesced around the new game plan and the new sheriff in town. We centered on a concise, well-understood turnaround and survival guide represented by the 1-Pager. To begin with a few counterproductive people had to be moved out. Then morale soared and everybody got on the same page of rebuilding. We came out of the legal crisis; hit our financial targets and many people got promoted and took on broader responsibilities—proof that people were growing, learning, and developing as a result of the 1-Pager. It's now a central tool in my leadership journey.

1-Paging in Action

By Josita Todd
Chief Information Officer
CMGI

Issue:

One Company I joined as CIO was very focused on five key strategies. The most important was sales force effectiveness for all five business units. My organization was expected to provide world-class IT support.

Before:

Each business unit owned its own resources and budgets. There were multiple e-mail systems, documentation systems, payroll, ERP, CRM, and Access databases across the organization. There were duplicated development efforts and resources with no leveraging of talent and IT assets. Bringing these business units together needed courage and focus.

1-Paging:

To start, we created a simple 1-Page Game Plan that mapped all IT-related initiatives in the business units to the five key strategies. If there was an initiative that did not map, then we challenged why we were doing it. We used the same 1-Pager to map cash and other resource allocation to the five key strategies on our dashboard. What we found was astonishing. We were spending upward of $60 million on IT-related initiatives and NOT ONE was focused on sales force effectiveness. They were all in operations.

After:

The 1-Pager enabled a complete realignment of our approach. As a result of the 1-Page Game Plan the VP of operations reduced the number of IT initiatives and funding was transitioned to the VP of sales. This had never happened in the history of the company! To this day, we still use it as an approach for focusing and budgeting all IT initiatives.

1-Paging Chapter Four

- 1-Paging leads to strong alignment when people can make a powerful personal connection between a goal and just how they are involved in its achievement.

- A _Strategy_ is a powerful, short, actionable, phrase that focuses people's minds on how a goal will be achieved. It generates a shared mental pathway in which activities will be carried out that cause the goal to be delivered.

- _Tactics_ are crisp descriptions of the specific activities to be carried out down the pathway. Each should have its own specific deliverables, time scale, and team member(s) accountable for execution.

- Strategies and tactics need to be renewed regularly in light of experience and progress shown on dashboards.

- Tactics get completed—or they fail to work or they get adapted. Revising and updating strategies, goals, and tactics is the ongoing work of the leadership team until the goals are fully accomplished.

CHAPTER FOUR

Strategies and Tactics

The mental and visual frameworks produced by 1-Paging solve so many of the pieces of the complex puzzle of leading myself and my team toward the vital few goals. You will sense such an increase in your potential when you work down the 1-Pager for the first time. From your inspiring vision statement at the top through to the goals and measures that describe what has to be delivered, you simply continue working down the page under each goal to crisply describe how you intend to achieve the goals.

1-PAGING SYMBOLS

STRATEGY

⇩

TACTICS

In 1-Paging parlance, we call how we plan to achieve our goals **Strategies** and **Tactics** and, yet again, it's back to basics and simplicity on the topics.

Defining Strategies and Tactics

A strategy is a powerful high-level statement of how we plan to get to the goal. Tactics are the series of clearly stated, connected steps executed to perform the strategy. That's why the arrow connects them on the template. For example, if you and I are wealthy owners of a professional football team, we might have the goal of winning the championship. A strategy of buying the best players is our way to achieve that goal, and the tactics are about finding the money, scouting, and then bidding on players and getting them fit and so on.

Here's the nugget:

> *It's your tactics that actually get executed to achieve your goal. It's your strategy phrase that holds the power to keep your mind focused on its achievement.*

For example, if your relationship goal is to strengthen your business team, then your strategy statement might say "Expand <u>every</u> single person's ability to contribute more," and the tactics would then be to evaluate each person, define each person's new assignments, execute their training, provide personal coaching support, and so on.

Completing the Game Plan

You can see my completed plan on the opposite page—the strategy and tactics boxes have been completed. As I build my 1-Pager, I work down the page, keeping the vertical alignment **Goal-Measure-Strategy-Tactics**.

Note that each tactic is a bullet point that is followed by someone's initials—my team member accountable—plus the expected date of completion (in this case by our fiscal quarter—Q1, Q2, etc.).

Remember that the 1-Pager is a <u>living</u> document used regularly in our 5-Questions review meetings. (Note: More on this process in the next chapter.) Goals and measures are updated occasionally, strategies more often, and tactics frequently, because they get completed or they simply need to be changed because they are not delivering the needed result.

My 1-Page Game Plan

Read down the page below each goal. Do my strategies help focus your mind on the tactics below?

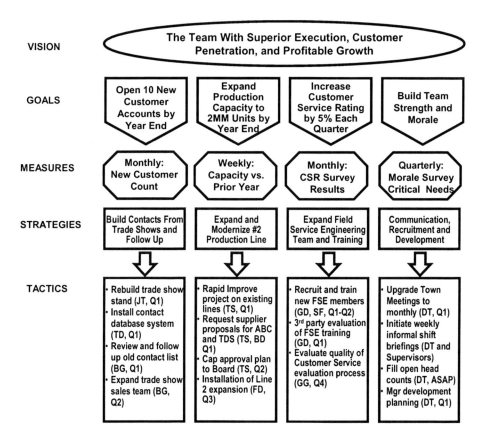

Strategies (Question 4: Does my direction need to change?)

Great strategies are phrased so clearly that they literally pull you in the direction of actionable tactics. In a team setting, debating the phrasing rapidly sets people in the right direction. I'm sometimes guilty of spending too much time trying to wordsmith the strategy statement and not enough time ensuring that the strategies are actually the best ones. Compare the phrases in the left and right columns in the table below and see how they lead you down different paths.

Strong Strategy Phrase	Weak Strategy Phrase
Recruit the best-ranked football players.	Find players that can score.
Expand the sales team with top performers.	Find better sales people.
Communicate results and issues to all employees.	Coordinate more employee meetings.

I strongly recommend spending time up front doing the necessary data gathering and research to create great strategies that inspire clarity and focus. It really pays off each time you ask Question 4.

True to my principle of keeping things simple, here is a nugget I uncovered when struggling to define the right strategy.

> *Likely, you are not the first person to have such a goal, so uncover a winning strategy by looking inside or outside your organization and rapidly adapting someone else's success formula.*

If you meet someone with prior experience, there's a very simple test of any strategy statement on your 1-Pager. You ask them this:

> "Can you help me, please? We plan to [*Insert Goal Statement*] by [*Insert Strategy Statement*]. Does this make sense to you; what steps would you recommend; and what pitfalls might we find?"

Of course, if you have in-depth experience of what works, then you will know the right strategy already, but be careful of the temptation to believe that you instinctively know the right strategy. Being wrong can be very expensive!

Tactics (Question 5: What must I now organize to get done?)

Tactics typed into the fifth layer of the template are simply a list of the work steps you plan to do in order to execute the strategy to achieve your goal. Many of them you will know from previous experience.

Question: What do you do when you don't know what tactics to do, and you can't find someone who has tried it before?

Answer: Use the Four-Step Process that follows.

Result: The tactics with the highest probability of success.

Remember that the 1-Page Game Plan is no different from any other basic management process—the quality of your output is a function of the quality of your input. So thinking time spent up front is a valuable investment. The Four-Step Process requires you to do some preliminary analysis so that the effort you invest in creating winning strategies and tactics is properly focused on the goal.

Four-Step Process for Strategies and Tactics

Step One: Get the Accountability or Relationship Goal Clear

We've covered this already. Remember that the key to clarity lies in thinking in terms of the outcome that will be delivered.

Step Two: Measure the Goal and the Gap

We've covered this before, too. Without a measurement system in place, we can't see if we are closing the gap between the goal and the starting baseline.

Step Three: The Critical-to-Quality Drivers of Success

Now the clever bit. This is where the investment in time and effort is needed. You have many options to achieve the result you want. You have to find the <u>cause-and-effect</u> relationships that are the most powerful in achieving the goal. Process improvement tools are very helpful in this analysis of what activity delivers the impact you want. From a potentially long list of possibilities, try to gather data in order to demonstrate the strength of the correlation, then you can move forward with greater confidence by selecting a path that has the highest probability of positively influencing the goal measurement (closing the gap). If you get new data, be prepared to adopt new strategies.

Step Four: Defining and Taking Action

Having used a cause-and-effect approach to selecting the right strategy, you can use the same method to ensure that the projects or solutions (tactics) you put in place are the right ones to deliver the strategy. It is a repeatable and highly effective process.

The cause-and-effect analysis in the Four-Step Process yields those strategies and tactics that you need to follow to achieve your accountability or relationship goal.

Here's a group of three nuggets on tactics:

1. *Get clear ownership for each tactic. Try not to share accountability among multiple people—it provides unintended hiding places when asking the 5-Questions.*

2. *Be as specific as possible on what needs to be delivered and by when for each tactic.*

3. *Involve both your team and partner organizations in developing the tactics. Failing to engage them produces barriers further down the road.*

There's a powerful side effect of the Four-Step Process, especially if it's done in a group setting. It builds confidence in the tactics you choose. And you need lots of confidence—you still need to execute them!

1-Paging Advice: Chapter Four

- Sometimes it's necessary to have multiple strategies for accountability or relationship goals. However, the best scenario is to work hard to identify just one strategy, the <u>winning</u> one, which unites everyone in achieving the goal.

- Intuition and your latest good idea won't yield the right strategies and tactics. There are tried-and-tested approaches for doing this that you should learn. The Four-Step Process based on Six Sigma principles is highly effective.

- Building the content of the 1-Page Game Plan should not be an exercise in wordsmithing. Everyone will want to be the editor but don't allow them to distract you. Focus on getting the right things on the page and appoint one person to own all the updating tasks in a team meeting.

- Having done a great job in populating the 1-Pager, don't forget to execute! Take a project management view with the help of the 5-Questions. **Execute—Measure—Renew—Execute**. Time spent defining project ownership, deliverables, and milestones up front, always pays handsome dividends later.

- When a tactic is completed, delete it from the 1-Pager fifth layer and craft a new one. Let your dashboard tell the story of your success, not your Game Plan. And don't forget to celebrate results.

1-Paging in Action

By Al Altomari
Chief Operating Officer
Barrier Therapeutics Inc.

Issue:

Barrier Therapeutics is an emerging bio-pharmaceutical organization. All the funding to date has come not from internal operations but through venture and public equity. As we started to commercialize drugs, we needed to launch a highly focused commercial organization capable of delivering on targeted goals with efficient use of funds.

Before:

The commercial organization I lead was the last function to be developed. From the time the decision was taken to build-out, we had to accelerate the implementation plan. It was critical that the corporate strategy, the commercial goals, and deliverables were "marbled" in the organization.

1-Paging:

Using a 1-Pager, we captured our corporate strategy (this was a four part strategy articulated in our public filings). We also captured the commercial strategies that are directly linked to our corporate strategies. Lastly, the key milestones and timing of these milestones were captured. To galvanize this in our culture, we had the commercial 1-Pager framed and on clear display in our office. Another approach we utilized was having every person on the commercial team develop their personal 1-Pager and dashboard for their own development. This step was critical so that all activities stay linked to the commercial 1-Pager and ultimately to the corporate strategy.

After:

After utilizing this "trickle down" one-page technique, the organization has become much more efficient. Staff meetings focus on dashboards, milestones, and execution. Ultimately, performance management is more streamlined since goals are clear and spelled out.

1-Paging Chapter Five

- *Even the simplest plan quickly becomes obsolete in today's complex world. To build a 1-Pager without anticipating this is like building a ship without expecting bad weather.*

- *Think again in terms of the <u>experience of alignment</u> of a team; if this experience is to have constancy and motivation, then it must be constantly re-created through the use of informal and formal <u>renewal events.</u>*

- *Informal renewal events are used to update the 1-Page Game Plan, such as in regular team meetings around the 5-Questions. This not only keeps the 1-Pager current, but it also repeatedly reinforces the key elements of focus in everyone's mind.*

- *Formally, we renew the 1-Page Game Plan along with Business Plans and Strategic Plans—they are part of the same integrated process in large organizations.*

- *By using the 1-Page Game Plan in this continuous way, any organization has the perfect tool to integrate planning and execution across multiple departments.*

CHAPTER FIVE

The Renewal Cycle

I've come to think of the 1-Pager as a management tool that benefits the core of my planning and execution activities. When I use it in a team setting with the 5-Questions, it's a very engaging, team-based mechanism for focus and alignment—a highly effective remedy for silo-based thinking. But in order for it to be truly successful, it must be continually worked on for the benefit of the entire organization.

The nugget that applies here is a jewel:

> *Your 1-Paging is not a one-off activity. Make it a continuous process for refreshing your motivation, alignment, and communication.*

Please don't ever think of your 1-Pager as finished. Its greatest power lies in its capability to be dynamic and adaptable enough to take account of changes in the environment without people losing focus or it taking weeks of effort to re-create.

When the 1-Pager stays relevant and up-to-date— often updated in real time through computer and projector—it grows into an amazing leadership alignment and communications tool.

The **Renewal Cycle** is the process I use to make sure the 1-Page Game Plan is part of my ongoing business activity. It's a method and structure, appropriate to my team and situation, that ensures we stay focused. It applies just as much to my major solo projects as my team goals.

You will need to create a team renewal cycle that is customized to your situation.

If you work largely solo or in a small organization, then your renewal effort may be nothing more than a weekly review and update of your plan and dashboard.

If you are in a large organization, the team renewal cycle looks very different. Remember this: 1-Paging is a cross-functional, enterprise-wide approach. If only partially deployed, it becomes sub-optimal and team motivation starts to break down.

Question: In complex team situations, how do we use the 1-Pager to avoid common business glitches caused by a breakdown in the linkages between team members or departments?

Answer: By creating a renewal cycle that involves all the people concerned with our project and our long-range business planning.

The simple 1-Pager format encourages the broad involvement of many individuals and departments concerned. So we involve them from the beginning of the planning process, and in all subsequent meetings—rather than presenting them with a *fait accompli*, as we often used to do. That way, they keep a clear impression of what they need to do to help us all be successful.

Clear communication is essential. In the 1-Pager we have a great vehicle to communicate our plans and, through our dashboards, show progress to everyone concerned.

Beware the Fate of "Corporate Initiatives"

If you come from a large organization, while I want you to be an advocate for, and user of, the 1-Paging approach, please try not to create the impression that you are embarking upon another corporate initiative. I know from experience that this is a certain turnoff for colleagues who are tired of new initiatives and are unlikely to welcome with open arms something they perceive to be draining their scarce time and energy. Haven't we all got enough to do as it is?

The key is not to create a completely separate or disconnected set of activities around the 1-Page Game Plan but, instead, to try to lock it firmly into the regular cycle of business planning and day-to-day business management.

In large organizations, this happens on two levels I call **Minor Renewal** and **Major Renewal.**

Minor Renewal – Part of Day-to-Day Business

In order to fully deploy the 1-Paging approach, it needs to be integrated into day-to-day management activities. For my team, the 1-Pager and dashboard actually forms the agenda for our meetings.

Here is the nugget on this topic:

> *Review the 1-Page Game Plan at meetings—then you get a perfect 5-Questions moment where you can stand back from all the hectic activity and ask: What has changed, why, and what will we do about it to stay aligned?*

Whenever we challenge the 1-Pager in this way, we ensure that our priorities are relevant and up-to-date. In the process of doing so, we also refresh and reinforce these priorities in our own minds. Plus we nip potential disruptions in the bud.

This does not mean spending excessive time reviewing the 1-Pager every week. What works well for me is a brief but systematic reflection at key meetings. It's just enough to keep the plan current while at the same time reinforcing the focus and alignment in my team. However, it needs disciplined commitment to take time to do it, otherwise the day-to-day issues become all-consuming.

Running Great 1-Paging Meetings

Have you ever been to a meeting where you were left wondering if any value had been added? Most likely the meeting ran out of time as well. I confess to having been to, and been in charge of, a few. We became consumed with the issue of the day. With the 1-Pager, these meetings are a thing of the past. How? By adopting the contents of the 1-Pager as the key agenda points for the meeting and using our dashboard as the data to drive decision making. Here's a recent example.

Meeting Title	Monthly Customer List Review
Meeting Objective	Assess progress against Goal 1 customer targets and take action where needed
Agenda Item 1	Review Monthly Customer Count Dashboard, including progress with key tactics.
Agenda Item 2	Determine actions needed to address any issues flagged by the Dashboard review – assign owners and target dates
Agenda Item 3	Review 1-Pager—ask 5-Questions, "What has changed and why?" and update game plan in real time.
Agenda Item 4	Summarize agreements, actions, and accountabilities from the meeting
Meeting Review	Take a moment to reflect on the meeting. Are we aligned? What can we do better next time?

By focusing our discussions on accountability and relationship goals, our dashboard, and the 5-Questions, we naturally address how we are doing and what action needs to be taken to stay on track. Long, drawn-out meetings are a thing of the past. I've actually reduced one daylong meeting to a couple of focused hours of work by keeping the dashboards up-to-date and action orientated.

Seems simple, doesn't it? Unfortunately, good intentions are never enough. Successful execution of our meetings, like the 1-Page Game Plan itself, requires a disciplined approach driven by a relentless desire to achieve our goals. We are helped by the fact that we know firsthand that the distraction demon is waiting to pounce. We try hard to stop distracting discussions before they de-focus us.

Major Renewal – Part of Business/Strategic Planning

The major renewal process, on the other hand, applies to large organizations and is more formal. It ensures that the outcomes of business and strategic planning processes are fully deployed.

Many organizations operate from the standpoint of needing long-term plans and, every planning period, financial forecasts. In our case, department long-term strategic plans tend to be done once a year so that all department plans can be aggregated and used for long-term planning and investment. Business planning, on the other hand, is frequently focused on quarter-to-quarter financial performance and kept separate. It helps the organization firm up sales and income forecasts and set budgets accordingly.

This conventional approach to strategic and business planning misses an enormous opportunity. If you start from the standpoint of wanting to focus the minds (and, subsequently, the actions) of people to achieve growth in performance, you end up building a continuous planning process that includes short-term and long-term considerations. Strategic and financial forecasts can then be spun off from this process whenever they are needed. Guess which management tool fits the bill?

The living 1-Pager fits it perfectly.

The 5-Questions apply from the top to the bottom of the organization, from the single individual to the mightiest CEO. What's different is the planning horizon—how far ahead you are trying to plan? With this refreshed view of accountability, you can adapt the framework.

Top-Down **and** Bottom-Up

My purpose here is to describe a process of crafting and renewing the 1-Pager in the broad context of growth of an entire business. Most organizations do this but lack the process to deploy the outcomes of the planning activity to the entire enterprise in a consistent and aligned manner that can have impact on short-term performance.

Traditionally, business planning tends to be done in a top-down manner. The targets of the management board are handed down to grateful departments that are often expected to "just do it." Yet this approach neglects the opportunity to involve stakeholders throughout the organization and empower people to deal with unplanned events that always occur.

What works best is a combination of top-down and bottom-up. This may sound complex, but, when you adopt the 1-Paging approach, it's incredibly straightforward once you take the time to learn how to do it.

The elements of the process are shown in the table.

Top-Down Elements ⟸⟹	Bottom-Up Elements
Reaffirmation by management board of the overall vision, business goals, and top-level 1-Pager and dashboard.	Local research and data gathering to create individual/ departmental goals, 1-Pager, and dashboard in cooperation with partners.
Environmental scan of marketplace and socioeconomic changes and definition of major investment initiatives for growth recorded on top-level 1-Pager.	Forming department and cross-functional teams to convert major and minor initiatives into tactics managed via 1-Pagers.
Guiding polices/principles for formulating goals, measures, strategies, tactics, formal renewal, and performance of departments and people.	Managing performance through departmental dashboards of measures, individual performance, informal renewal, and upward progress reporting.
Overall calendar/timetable of business/strategic plans, companywide communication of top-level performance, and hot issues.	Departmental meetings around 1-Pager, hot issues, coordinating employee meetings, and input to top-level business/strategic plans.

Ownership of the Major Renewal Cycle

The most important nugget for people considering using the 1-Pager throughout a large organization is this:

> *Make sure your 1-Paging process includes both PLANNING and progress in EXECUTION so that focus is not lost.*

For the process to be truly engaging and cross-functional, and for the entire organization to experience alignment, ultimate ownership for the renewal cycle must rest with the senior leadership team. Their acceptance of ownership of a top-down and bottom-up process is key to success. After all, in this age of complex team structures, who else can ensure <u>full</u> integration of the 1-Page Game Plan into regular work habits?

But, again, be careful of corporate initiatives. The planning process you build around the 1-Page Game Plan should be lean. It needs to be focused on getting the organization where it has to go, not off down another track. Making this happen can often be helped by appointing a respected editor for the enterprise-wide crafting and deployment. The editor must have credibility in the organization, be capable of strategic thinking (ideally with strong process orientation), and be concerned with overall 1-Pager content and accurate dashboards rather than wordsmithing.

I learnt my lessons on the importance of renewal back in the early days of my 1-Paging. As I mentioned earlier, we had great success initially in getting senior leaders to pull together their first 1-Pager. We even got them to commit to fully deploy the 1-Pagers to their global teams and use it as the basis for running meetings and tracking progress. I thought the job was done. Then, some months later, I noticed that while managers had pinned the 1-Pager on their office wall like a trophy, they were no longer using it to run the business. The business was losing focus again and the 1-Paging process risked becoming stale and redundant.

This was the point at which we took the 1-Pager off the wall and started bringing it into the existing planning and performance management processes. Rapidly, we got the sustained benefit we were after.

1-Paging Advice: Chapter Five

- Expect your 1-Page Game Plan to change. 1-Paging is not a one-off activity. The greatest power is in its capability to be dynamic and flexible enough to take account of changes in the environment in which you operate.

- In order to successfully deploy the 1-Pager, ensure that it is fully integrated with your structure or the way that work is actually done in you organization. The purpose is to help focus the organization to achieve more, not to add the burden of a new management tool.

- Don't let your weekly or monthly meetings be derailed by discussing all the items on the 1-Pager. Be selective, use your dashboard, and pick the high-impact issues that need attention.

- Use 1-Paging as a change-management tool at both management team and employee communication meetings. In both, take the opportunity to do some "minor renewal" of the 1-Pager by talking about what has changed, what will change, and what we all need to do about it.

- If you work the renewal of the 1-Page Game Plan into your organization's business planning and strategic planning processes, commit to see things through. The payoff is huge, but it can take a few planning cycles to emerge.

1-Paging in Action

By Alan Morgan
General Manager
MDS Clinical Development Services

Issue:

With more than 1,000 staff in 25 countries, it was hard to mobilize our employees to march in a single direction. We were losing staff, and there was no compelling vision as to why they should stay.

Before:

The management team was responding by simply dealing with mini crisis after mini crisis. We lacked proactivity, and this was compounded by the fact that we were regionally structured in a market that was increasingly global. Staff turnover was increasing, and this was negatively impacting new business authorizations as well as operating efficiency.

1-Paging:

The initial draft of the 1-Page Game Plan was the breakthrough we needed to globalize our business philosophy and get the whole team marching in a single direction with conviction. Refinements over the next two months really secured senior management support, and we gave copies to every employee and used the document to explain to key clients how we were committed to continuous improvement. It took us an additional year of continuous use before we really developed the tool to link to our metrics dashboard—it's getting better all the time.

After:

Giving a copy to every employee was the cement that held the strategy together—it was posted on office walls and cubicles around the world. The management team could not escape the commitments we signed up for. Turnover fell, operating performance improved, and new business authorizations turned the corner. We now use it throughout my organization in a top-down and bottom-up way.

1-Paging in Action

By Fred Gomberg
Vice President
Vertis Communications

Issue:

In my sales role, I'm largely a solo performer. I was spending way too much time each week on day-to-day small fires and small opportunities. I was not growing my business.

Before:

As each day started, my agenda was set by whoever got to me first with their issue of the day—whatever they felt the most important to address. I was not able to go forward and grow new opportunities. The pipeline was going dry. I was spending more time reworking past programs and other people's projects and not growing new business opportunities.

1-Paging:

I set up a list of four major goals I needed to reach. I was able to 1-Page what had to be done and how I was going to go about getting it done. A time frame was included for me to reach each goal. I made sure there were dashboards in place so I was able to see the progress I was making each week. I now had clear major priorities that I had to address first _before_ handling others' priorities.

After:

The 1-pager focused me on what I needed to do each day. It helped me get closer to my defined goals and pull back to let others work with their own situation. Before too long, I had to increase my goals and shorten timelines. My new client list grew and so had my business.

The 1-Pager continues to help me in putting goals in writing, creating a written plan, checking the progress, making adjustments, and having the right priorities. Staying focused is staying successful.

1-Paging Chapter Six

■ *We should all spend some time thinking through our personal goals in life, and how we can achieve them. We do it at work, so why not for our home life? The 1-Paging approach provides us with the perfect mechanism.*

■ *By thinking through our personal goals and strategies we can stay focused on what is truly important. We can frequently ask the 5-Questions at a personal level to ensure we are staying on track.*

■ *Personal changes happen as fast as professional ones. The 1-Paging approach helps us to stand back from time to time and revisit our longer-term personal aims and objectives. The renewal part of the 5-Questions applies here, too.*

■ *Arguably, a personal 1-Pager requires even more discipline to execute than a work-related version. Sharing the content of your personal 1-Pager with trusted family, friends, and advisers is very helpful. The very act of sharing will greatly increase the chances of achievement.*

CHAPTER SIX

Personal 1-Page Game Plan

This is a new spin on the topic often referred to as **Work/Life Balance**. If we are able to focus and align around key goals in a workplace setting, then why not apply the same thinking to our personal lives?

We all have personal aims and desires, be they health, wealth, pursuit of happiness or all three. In reality, these personal aims are the outcomes we strive for. In 1-Paging parlance, they are our accountability and relationship goals, but in simple terms they are merely what we are striving to achieve in life from the standpoint of career, health, family and friends.

Consciously and unconsciously we all regularly think about how to achieve these personal things. In other words, we are trying to figure out our personal strategies and tactics. I want to lose 14 pounds in the next six weeks; how will I do it? If I want to be promoted to the next level in the organization, what steps should I take? If I want to secure my children's education, how will I finance it?

Can you see the fit with the principles of 1-Paging? These personal goals are begging for a dashboard, a strategy, and some tactics.

Why Bother With a Personal Plan?

At first glance, it seems like overkill, almost like bringing work home, to go to the trouble of writing down a personal 1-Pager. Yet there are good reasons why each of us should have a 1-Pager to help guide our private lives. The distraction demon is there just the same, if not worse, than at work. And the very act of thinking through some personal strategies and tactics encourages me—and my family—to get focused on "what is important to us all around here."

Of course, we also frequently ask our version of the 5-Questions to ensure we stay on track. Please don't underestimate the power of this personal discipline. It helps us to determine what we need to do to achieve what we are aiming for. What's more, the sense of alignment for an individual or family is even more gratifying than at work.

Why do I take the trouble of doing this? Because I care enough to commit to achieving something important for my family, and I feel we owe it to ourselves to try to get there.

A Personal One-Page Game Plan

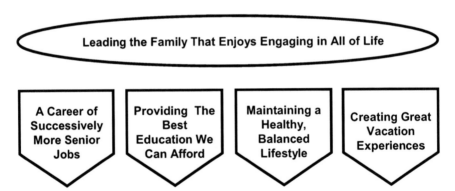

Of course, none of this is inconsistent with my principle of keeping to basics, neither in a professional or personal setting, but it is amazing the results that this straightforward and disciplined approach can bring.

It helps to stand back from the hectic world we live in, both at work and at home, and gets focused on the vital few things that really make a difference. In doing so, we get a real sense of progress, and we bring focus to the frantic activity that distracts us from what is truly important.

Our first nugget on this topic:

> *The principles involved in the attainment of personal and professional goals are identical—clear direction, consistency of purpose, laser-guided focus, and a road map for how to get there.*

Therefore, you can use the simple 1-Pager layout and templates to achieve this very quickly.

The Renewal Cycle at Home

If people balk at the idea of committing to paper their personal set of strategies and tactics, then they absolutely revolt when it comes to the idea of applying the 5-Questions and renewal. They argue that they are on top of life and can safely leave 1-Paging at work.

Yes, renewal also applies at home! We need a mechanism to stand back from all that is going on and refresh in our own minds what is relevant and important. By adopting the 1-Pager in our private lives we stay tuned to changing circumstances and adapt our strategies to our changing life circumstances.

In my first job I worked as a planning engineer for a major electronics company, where I was responsible for routing product through the shop floor. On the first day in my job I was invited to meet with the divisional director in charge of our business unit. I expected him to give me the usual stuff about the company and how I would do well if I worked hard.

However, I was surprised by what he told me. Having welcomed me to the company, he went on to explain his philosophy for career progression. He insisted that a percentage of my time should be devoted to working on my personal aims. He told me that I should know six months ahead of time what my next move would be, so that I could plan how to get there.

"Nobody will do this for you," he said, "It's up to you to make your life happen".

It was years later that I realized 1-Paging is the perfect accompaniment to the philosophy he suggested. It causes you to refresh your professional and personal goals, to think through how you will get there, and regularly check how you are doing with people you trust. It is a great personal planning and execution tool.

Commitment—Sharing Your 1-Pager

Personal 1-Pagers are even harder to sustain than the ones at work, and it goes against the grain for me to indulge in this type of formality for personal planning. It is even more far-fetched to contemplate committing personal aims to paper, or even sharing them with family or friends. Yet the act of sharing these things drives a higher level of personal commitment to follow-through.

This nugget is about personal accountability.

> ***Tell people you trust what you really aim to achieve professionally and personally—it makes it far more likely you will actually do it.***

Now, nobody is suggesting that a personal 1-Page Game Plan needs to be a beautifully designed presentation, beamed to an eager family in the living room every Saturday evening. That is not something your average 1-Paging exponent would recommend!

The approach needs to be more subtle but can have a tremendous impact. Just talking about it helps, asking the basic questions in everyday language. How am I doing in my quest to lose 14 pounds (my goal)? Have I been doing the things I said I would, like eating the right foods and keeping up the exercise regime (my tactics)?

Another nugget for you, this time about forming your **Personal Board of Directors**:

> *If not family or friends, then pick several people you trust who can act as unofficial "coaches" or "mentors," with whom you can review the 1-Pager and 5-Questions.*

This type of coaching support is increasingly available at work, so why not at home too?

None of the above implies that 1-Paging should somehow take over your life. Similarly, there are plenty of self-help books available. The 1-Pager should be viewed as a simple and useful process for keeping you organized to achieve your aims, a tool to be revisited when a "touch on the tiller" is needed.

If you have children, try it with them.

1-Paging Advice: Chapter Six

- You sometimes forget that some of the useful tools available at work can also help at home. In the 1-Page Game Plan you have a simple and useful tool that can be flexibly applied in either setting. Start by sharing your work 1-Pager with your family.

- There is no need to tell anyone that you have a personal 1-Pager, but it is important that you discuss the content—the goals, dashboard, and tactics—with people who can support you.

- Don't view the personal 1-Pager as a formal or rigid tool. View it instead as a thought process, a great way of getting organized to get things done. You can use it for as many projects as you need.

- Make sure you set aside time to renew your personal 1-Pager. Forgetting to do this is certain evidence that you let the fuzziness and distraction demons rule your life.

1-Paging in Action

By Cynthia Lyons
Staffing Consultant
Forrest Solutions

Issue:
As a young adult I wanted to maximize as many financial and personal avenues to enhance my overall life. This included savings.

Before:
I did not have any clear system of investing or saving my earnings. I also did not know much about investing. I knew I wanted to become more in my job but was not sure how to make that happen. While I was utilizing my friends as networking contacts, I was not getting out of my comfort zone and exploring different options or leveraging my existing professional relationships.

1-Paging:
I created a clear personal 1-Page plan that included clear actions to take and milestones to get to my overall goals. I set weekly and monthly goals and created a personal board of directors for me to turn to for guidance and advice. I now touch base monthly with my personal board of directors to go over my progress and monitor any obstacles I may be facing. I send them my updated personal 1-Pager before each conversation.

After:
I like the feeling of being accountable to my board of directors. Instead of thinking about my goals, I am acting upon them. Due to a clearer understanding of what I want, I was able to speak with my manager and express my desires at work—the result: a management role. I now know what needs to be done on a weekly basis in order to make my long-term goals happen. In regards to my finances, I now have a direction to go in order to get more information and learn more about investing. I am not overwhelmed by the prospect of investing and growing my clientele. In a nutshell, I'm so happy that my personal goals are now manageable and possible.

1-Paging.com
Download Templates

Level 1 Template: *Each Goal Has One Strategy*

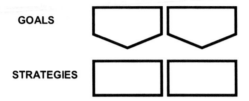

Level 2 Template: *Goals Have Multiple Strategies*

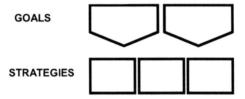

Level 3 Template: *Each Goal Has*
Critical-to-Quality Strategies

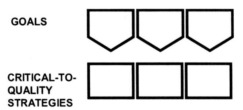

CHAPTER SEVEN

Picking the Right Template

1-Paging.com is there to help you with all your projects, no matter what your level of experience may be.

Since I'm a great believer in simply not reinventing things, particularly when others have had great success with these tools, I should point out that the downloadable templates, dashboards, and other items at www.1-Paging.com are adapted from living versions of the 1-Pager.

Your journey in using the 1-Paging approach will always be just that—a journey. The 1-Pager is a focusing, planning, and communicating tool that you and your team will learn to use with ever-increasing levels of sophistication. Starting at the right place and taking full advantage of the experience of others are both very important.

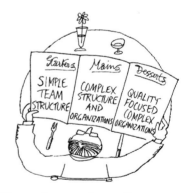

There are three levels of templates available for you to download—simple, complex and quality-focused complex. Each download includes a 1-Paging template, some instructions, the 5-Questions, and an example of a completed template. You can build your 1-Pager in a variety of ways.

Circumstances vary so much that it's impossible to create a universal template for dashboards; however the website does include examples and many other helpful 1-Paging templates for you.

Level 1—Simple Team Structures

If you work mostly alone, or if you run a small business or department and this is your first experience in developing a strategic plan, the Level 1 template fits perfectly.

Even if you think your world is incredibly complex, I still suggest you try Level 1 first. Remember that the 1-Pager is also a communication tool, and simplicity works best when it comes to learning to align diverse groups of people.

The Level 1 template is the one you have been seeing throughout the earlier chapters of this book. It has a direct relationship from top to bottom—each accountability or relationship goal box has one measure box, one strategy box, and one list of tactics.

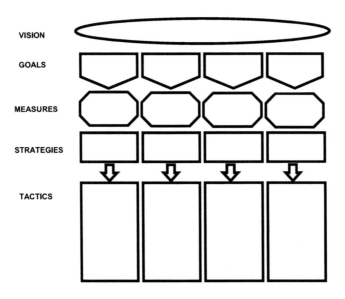

Let me reiterate that, in a team situation, you should be careful of grabbing the template and rushing to complete your team's game plan on your own.

The primary purpose is to focus and align you and your team, and that means involving them and other important partners in the 1-Pager creation process. If you are beginning the process, set up a series of meetings and start with the 5-Questions, the definitions of the core elements of the plan, and your ideas for the top-level items. Then, expect the plan to become a living document, constantly being updated and communicated by your team. It really helps to appoint one member of your team to be the updater and custodian of the latest version and dashboard.

Level 2—Complex Structures and Organizations

If you lead a large, geographically diverse team or organization, you may already realize that there is seldom a one-to-one relationship between a goal and the strategy for achieving it on the 1-Pager. For example, sales growth may come from a strategy of hiring better salespeople, <u>and</u> a strategy of equipping them with better market support.

Where there are multiple strategies for achieving your goals in this way, start with the Level 2 Template, which enables these multiple goal-strategy relationships.

Another major difference between Level 1 and Level 2 is that the measures are not recorded on the game plan; you will need to create a second page defining your dashboard of measures for each goal or strategy. Just keep it simple.

Here is the layout of the Level 2 template. Notice that there are more strategies than goals.

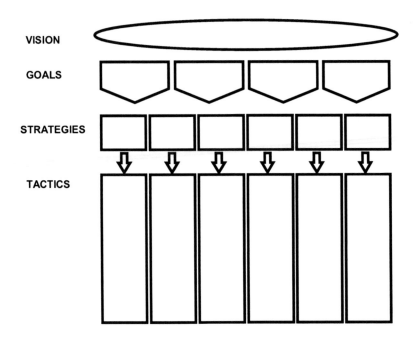

The Level 2 template is an excellent tool for teams that plan and report their goals and dashboards in a group setting—face-to-face or electronically.

For the process to be truly engaging and cross-functional, cascade this template down and across your organization by asking team members/partners to complete their own 1-Pager. Do this by entering the vision statement and goals only, and then have them complete their own strategies and tactics to fit your top-level entries. Finally, meet and watch the misalignment sparks fly as you go through the process of building a coherent cross-functional picture in everyone's mind. Don't expect to get alignment in just one session. Focusing is not always pain-free.

The opposite page shows a completed Level 2 Game Plan with four goals and six strategies kindly provided by an experienced 1-Paging user.

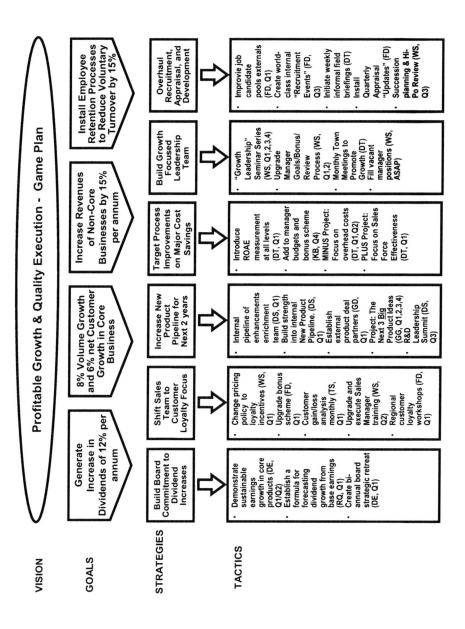

Level 3—Quality-Focused Complex Organizations

If you run a complex, diverse team and your team members are experienced in process improvement methodologies like Six Sigma, you will find Level 3 to be your ideal starting point.

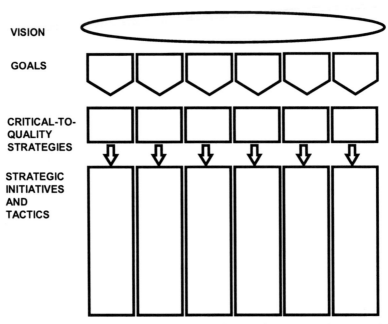

You know already that there are many alternative strategies to achieve your goals. The issue is finding the critical few that are best.

The Four Step process for arriving at the best strategies and tactics is covered in Chapter 4. It's where an investment in time and effort is used to reveal the cause-and-effect relationships that are the most powerful in achieving a goal. It's this analysis that leads to the Critical-to-Quality Strategies that you place on the Level 3 template.

This cause and effect analysis provides enormous benefit to the development of the 1-Pager and the subsequent meetings at which it is updated.

GOAL — Expansion Portfolio of Clients by 20% in All Segments

CRITICAL-TO-QUALITY STRATEGIES —
- Double win rates
- Develop new value-added service
- Leverage existing client relationships

There is an important nugget of a question implicitly asked each time you review the Level 3 1-Pager:

> *Are we constantly focusing our efforts on those few strategies we believe are critical to top performance?*

The following page is a completed Level 3 template kindly provided by an experienced 1-Paging user. Notice how the simple vertical alignment lost in Level 2 is now retrieved at Level 3.

VISION: The Innovative, Reliable, and Consistent Provider of Services

	Deepen Therapeutic Expertise Reputation	Achieve World Class in Project Management	Drive OM of 12% with Revenue Growth of 18% per annum	Develop Leadership Throughout Organization	Expansion Portfolio of Clients by 20% in all Segments
CRITICAL-TO-QUALITY STRATEGIES	• Launch new therapeutic areas with global impact • Back up launches with real expertise • Measure reputation	• Measure our reputation for PM • Smartest PM tools • Experienced PM recruits hungry to expand tools	• Quality sales opportunity system • Six-Sigma Process re-engineering • New pricing on value-add services	• Develop and retain existing top talent • Recruitment focus: NA PMs • Effective appraisals to stretch individuals	• Double win rates • Develop new value-added service • Leverage existing client relationships
STRATEGIC INITIATIVES AND TACTICS	• Launch Therapeutic Area 2 with dedicated team (DP) • Expand Therapeutic Area 1 into Europe via point person in Europe (MM) • Leverage Medicaid expertise into Europe (BL) • Hire 6 PMs with specific Therapeutic Areas 2 & 3 background by Q3 (ML/MG) • Plan & Launch Therapeutic Area 3 by Q4 (DP)	• Initiate biannual survey of our PM performance, quality of tools, and reputation staring in Q2 (CF) • PM Tools evaluate, enrich, train, and follow up (DG) • 6 world-class recruits from competitors against the "PM Career" competence profile (CF)	• Re-engineer 3 target processes using Lean Sigma (AM) • World class grants and pass-throughs (DH) • Implement value added services (SP) • Contract Mgt to identify, isolate, and address low performing (GW) • EVA variance reporting for top 50 projects by Q2 (DS)	• Intensify all staff communications processes (GS, All) • Recruitment focus upon NA Project Management – see Goal 2 • 100% compliance to annual appraisal process to drive stretch personal objectives (GS, All)) • Manage leadership development via succession planning assignments from Q1 (GS) • Training records on system by Q1 (GS)	• Install bid optimization process in Q1 (GW) • Lessons learned meeting for all major losses (GW) • Exec attendance at every bid defense (All) • Expand medical and regulatory presence in California Biotech (SP/BH) • Scorecard review - escalation process for red projects (SE) (DB)

Advice of 1-Paging Users

We surveyed active users for advice to include here. We found a high level of consistency. These are the top three responses for each question.

1. **What is your primary purpose in using the 1-Page Game Plan in your organization?**
   a. Consolidating key areas of focus for my team.
   b. Driving results through clarity of purpose for me and my team.
   c. Communicating business priorities across the organization.

2. **Which elements do you consider to be most critical to the successful deployment of the 1-Page Game Plan?**
   a. Investing in time to craft relevant and actionable content.
   b. Integrating the Game Plan updating into the regular management process.
   c. Involving the right people in the process.

3. **How is deployment of the 1-Page Game Plan tied to day-to-day management processes?**
   a. Functional and process 1-Pagers are cascaded throughout the organization.
   b. Used at meetings to set agendas.
   c. Formally integrated with business planning and execution tracking system.

4. **How do you measure progress and renew the 1-Pager?**
   a. We update the Game Plan quarterly or annually from dashboards.
   b. We update the game plan as a team activity.
   c. We measure achievement at the goal level.

5. **What are the most important reasons for failure when deploying a 1-Page Game Plan throughout your organization?**
   a. Lack of integration with day-to-day leadership and management of the business.
   b. Poor follow-up/execution and laziness in updating.
   c. Lack of integration with business planning.

6. **What specific advice would you give to others starting to build and adopt a 1-Page Game Plan approach?**

   a. Ensure the process is part of overall business planning. Don't allow it to be viewed as a separate activity. Focus on the vital few things and assign clear ownership.

   b. Don't get hung up on wordsmithing, because this can have a paralyzing rather than energizing effect. Try to keep it simple; there will be a temptation to overload.

   c. Maintain a high level of engagement, keep concise and meaningful. Construct with the leadership team. Use it regularly.

   d. Make sure you understand and get buy-in on the business vision and key strategic goals.

   e. Avoid multiple tools for planning strategy and development of plans. Stick with the basics and an understandable philosophy.

   f. Work from the top down to drive the vision and leadership of senior management into the organization and to align the business with the vision.

   g. Take the time to really think about the specific goals and objectives that are driving your growth.

   h. Keep it simple; make it a "living document."

CHAPTER EIGHT

Closing Remarks

Congratulations! If you learn to master any of the 1-Pager templates, the distraction demon will surely be conquered. You will be distilling your goals, strategies, and tactics onto a single page in a manner that can uplift and galvanize an entire global organization. Not only will your team be aligned, but you will also have the simple means to integrate other departments and colleagues should you need to.

Remember that it is not just the action of writing everything on a single page that helps achieve goals. The real value is in systematically bringing together all the input needed to <u>sustain</u> focus and follow-up. By using the 1-Pager on a day-to-day basis to stay on track, and by periodically asking the 5-Questions, you will refresh and renew the plan, keeping it relevant and up-to-date in everyone's mind. When the distraction demon knocks, corrective action will never be far off.

In summary, 1-Paging will bring you success when you are:

Focusing your plan succinctly onto 1-Page.

Communicating your 1-Page confidently to get rapid alignment with your team.

Renewing your 1-Page Game Plan through the 5- Questions that keep a sharp focus.

Executing your 1-Page plan, reporting progress, and running meetings with the same disciplined focus.

You know already that 1-Paging has brought success to me and to the 1-Paging users that have provided their 1-Paging in Action reports. 1-Paging delivers across a broad range of situations—from a solo project to running a global corporation.

1-Paging is truly an area that can be improved by learning from the hands-on experience of others, so we want your good ideas as to how to make the 1-Pager work. Please visit www.1-Paging.com and share your developments with other users.

And, stay focused, celebrate your achievements, and enjoy the journey!

1-Paging.com

Acknowledgments

To the 1-Paging users everywhere—the real creators of this work—we owe an enormous debt of gratitude. (From Stephen: This includes you, Alan!) You have taken the 1-Paging concept and brought it to life in your business and personal lives, and willingly shared your developments with others. We are especially grateful to those users who have contributed their experiences in the 1-Paging in Action reports, and User Survey. Thank you from the bottom of our hearts to:

    Al Altomari, Barrier Therapeutics Inc.
    Bill Cordivari, formerly of Ortho Dermatological (J&J)
    Don Deieso, EduNeering Inc.
    Fred Gomberg, Vertis Inc.
    Peter Gray, ICON Clinical Research Plc.
    Terry Herring, inVentiv Commercial Services
    Cynthia Lyons, Forrest Solutions Inc.
    Michael McNamara, Neutrogena Inc.
    Alan Morgan, MDS Inc.
    David O'Keeffe, Bard Inc.
    Willie Printie, LifeScan Ltd.
    Mark Roskey, Caliper Life Sciences Inc.
    Josita Todd, CMGI

Other leaders have graciously reviewed the manuscript. Our thanks especially for the outstanding specific contributions of Tim Cumming, Christopher Dowie, Jonathan Dowie, Monique Easley, Tony Flaherty, Dana Hyland George, Martyn Lee, Gary Stine, and Jim Walters.

We must also add special thanks to Sam Smith for the great cartoons, Lisa Marien for the cover design, both Dana Hilmer and Judy Pilone for their excellent editing skills, and Brian Hasenkamp at Asenka Creative Services for the 1-Paging.com logo and web site.

And last, and far from least, to our wives and families. Their support for us during our collaboration has been our strength.

Printed in the United States
201271BV00003B/172-366/P